THE LIFE OF A KENTUCKY COLONEL

Things you may not have known about Harlan Sanders' unordinary life, success in business, and genuine faith in Christ.

Copyright © 2020 by Edward DeVries

ISBN: 9798683170127

Published by:
Dixie Heritage Press
www.dixieheritage.net

INTRODUCTION

Before it became one of the world's largest fast food franchises, and before it was popular to have fast food franchises in gas stations, what we now know as Kentucky Fried Chicken, began as a small restaurant in the gas station of a Kentucky man named Harland Sanders.

Sanders died on December 16, 1980 at the age of 90. Forty years later, he remains the face of Kentucky Fried Chicken and the company's "mascot." His photograph and image are everywhere. And twenty years into the 21st Century, Colonel Harlan Sanders remains one of the world's most instantly recognizable faces.

The Colonel's life story, includes a lot more than just chicken.

Was Harlan Sander's really a Colonel? Yes, he was.

Was he a Mormon? No, he was not. Though one of his early business partners and franchisees was a Mormon.

Was he a man of faith? Yes, he was.

This brief eBook will tell the story of Harlan Sander's military service, the unusual rise of his restaurant empire, and how a lifelong "religious" man came to genuine faith in Christ in his late seventies.

TABLE OF CONTENTS

Chapter 1
A Simple Soldier Achieves the Rank of Colonel

Harlan Sanders falsified his birth date in order to enlist in the U.S. Army in 1906. His military service was uneventful. Much of it was served in post Spanish-American war Cuba. He was honorably discharged. As far as I can gather, he never rose beyond the rank of Private.

In 1935, Governor Ruby Laffoon issued a ceremonial decree commissioning Sanders as an "honorary Kentucky Colonel." He would receive a second such honorary commission from then- governor Earle Chester Clements in 1949.

For unknown reasons, Sanders embraced the title in 1949, changing his appearance to "look the part" by growing facial hair and donning a black frock coat and string tie. Soon after, "The Colonel" switched to a white suit, because it helped to hide flour stains. He also bleached his mustache and goatee to match his white hair.

Chapter 2
After the Army and Before Success

Before his success in the restaurant business Harlan Sanders had a very interesting résumé.

Upon leaving the Army he worked as a farmhand before landing a job as a streetcar conductor. That got him a job on the railroad and he bounced around, working for railroad companies across the South. Finally, he ended up settling for a time in Arkansas.

Before the "gig-economy" was even a thing, the young Sanders made extra money by delivering babies in Arkansas. He was not a doctor. But as he would write in his autobiography, "The husbands couldn't afford a doctor when their wives were pregnant."

With the money that Sanders earned delivering babies, he ordered correspondence courses in law, received his degree, and practiced briefly in rural justice-of-the-peace courts. His short legal career ended upbruptly in a courtroom brawl.

Moving to Kentucky, Sanders operated a steamboat ferry that crossed the Ohio River between Kentucky and Indiana. He also sold life insurance and automobile tires. The tire business helped him to establish his own gas station in Corbin, Kentucky.

A respected small businessman in Corbin, Sanders once again took on the job of delivering babies. "There was nobody else to do it," Sanders wrote in his autobiography.

Chapter 3
Gas Station Chicken

Nowadays, it is very common for gas stations to have fast-food and restaurant franchises within. But such was not the case back in 1930, when Harland Sanders first began to serve meals to truck drivers and motorists from a table in the front of his Shell Oil gas station in Corbin, Kentucky.

Fried chicken, however, was not originally on the menu because it took too long to prepare.

The signature dishes at Sander's gas station were ham and steak dinners. They were so popular that within a few years Sanders had enough money to open Sanders' Café across the street.

By 1935 fried chicken prepared in a cast-iron skillet and coated in a secret recipe of 11 herbs and spices had been added to the menu because food critic Duncan Hines included the restaurant and its chicken in his ***1935 Road-Food Guide***.

But the chicken still took too long to prepare. So Sanders was always experimenting with faster ways to fry his popular chicken. In 1939 he tried using a pressure cooker. The result was "heavenly."

To this day, Kentucky Fried Chicken is cooked in a pressure cooker which very quickly seals

in the juices of the meat and the flavor of The
Colonel's secret recipe.

Chapter 4
Temper Almost Cost Him Everything

The Young Harlan Sanders was a "hothead." And he never backed down from a fight. Just as his law career was lost to a courtroom brawl, The Colonel's chicken business was almost forever lost to a gunfight.

Harlan Sanders' Shell Oil gas station was right in the middle of a rough-and-tumble neighborhood known then as "Hell's Half-Acre." To advertise the business, and the food that it served, Sanders had painted giant advertising signs on barns for miles around. His aggressive advertising campaign had angered Matt Stewart, who owned a nearby Standard Oil gas station. Stewart decided to paint over one Sanders' signs. Sander's repainted and Stewart painted over it again. So Sanders and a cuple of executives from Shell Oil went to pay Mr. Stewart a visit. Stewart pulled a gun and fatally shot Shell district manager Robert Gibson. Sanders returned fire with his own pistol, wounding Stewart in the shoulder.

Both Sanders and Stewart were arrested. Sanders' charges would be dropped shortly after his arrest. Stewart was found guilty of murder and served 18 years in prison.

Chapter 5
Why Some Think He Was a Mormon

At age 65, Colonel Sanders retirement didn't turn out as well as he had planned. The highway department had relocated the highway to a new location nearly 7 miles away. What was once a major highway with a lot of traffic was now a local road that saw virtually no traffic whatsoever. Sander's Shell and his restaurant were bankrupt. The Colonel and his wife were living on his a $105-a-month Social Security check.

An aged, but still ambitious Colonel was now driving a 1946 Ford around the country teaching restaurants how to pressure cook fried chicken in hopes to enlist them as franchisees for his failing restaurant business.

The first Kentucky Fried Chicken franchise was established in Salt Lake City, Utah. It was purchased by Pete Harman, a Mormon businessman who at that time owned one of the city's largest restaurants.

It was Pete who suggested to Sanders the name "Kentucky Fried Chicken." The reason being to distinguish Sanders'/Harman's product from the "southern fried chicken" on so many restaurant menus. Pete also created the now famous bucket container.

Pete Harmon was a devout Mormon who used his connection in the Mormon Church to help Sanders sell franchises across the United States and even in foreign countries.

Chapter 6
Sanders Sells and Sues

At age 74, The Colonel would sell his Kentucky Fried Chicken Corporation for $122 million to a group of Mormon businessmen. Colonel Sanders would remain the public face and mascot of the company and its advertising.

Not wanting to retire, Sanders and his wife opened "The Colonel's Lady's Dinner House," in Shelbyville, Kentucky. The year was 1968.

The food conglomerate Heublein purchased Kentucky Fried Chicken Corporation in 1971. They too retained Sanders as the companies face and spokesperson.

Shortly after Heublein had acquired the chain, The Colonel walking into a Kentucky Fried Chicken restaurant for lunch. Thinking the gravy tasted like "slop," Sanders set out on a national tour of Kentucky Fried Chicken locations. In each, he was very disappointed in the food's taste and quality.

He tried to express his concerns to the new owners that the quality of the product was well below par and was basically told to shut up. So Sanders began publicly calling the Heublein management "a bunch of booze hounds." He also sued them for a familiar sum of $122 million dollars. They settled out of court for a mere $1 million and also agreed that Sanders would oversee a national training program giving cooking lessons to Heublein executives and franchise owners/managers. Sanders also agreed not to publicly criticize Heublein or Kentucky Fried Chicken. in return for his promise to stop criticizing Kentucky Fried Chicken's food. "The Colonel's Lady's Dinner House" was also renamed "Claudia Sanders Dinner House." That restaurant, at the time of this writing, is still open for business.

Chapter 7
The Southern Gentleman?

The Colonel may have appeared to be the beau-ideal of a Southern gentleman. But for most of his life, his language was anything but.

Harlan Sanders swore like a sailor, especially when he wasn't pleased with the quality of food served up by his franchisees.

In 1970, *New Yorker* magazine reported that, "The Colonel is famous among KFC people for the force and variety of his swearing."

In his autobiography, Sanders wrote, "I used to cuss the prettiest you ever heard...I did my cussin' before women or anybody else, but somehow nobody ever took any offense."

At the end of his life, when speaking to the students at Southern Seminary in Louisville, The Colonel said: "But all this while I knew I wasn't right with God. It bothered me especially when I'd take the name of the Lord in vain. I did my cussin' before women or anyplace. ... I knew the terrible curse of cussin' would probably keep me out of heaven when I died."

He would conclude his comments by saying, "when I asked the Lord to help me stop cussin' ... I lost half of my vocabulary."

Chapter 8
The Colonel Meets Christ

Just because he swore like a sailor did not mean that Harlan Sanders was not a religious man.

His father died when he was five-years-old. So he did not remember much about hlm. But he did remember that mother was a "God-fearing woman." Sanders would write, "We went to Sunday School every Sunday regardless of weather. We walked there and back two and a half miles."

He grew up believing that, "The Lord kept me on earth either to use me or punish me."

In his Army service he was faithful to attend the Chaplain's services. As an adult he was faithful to attend church and to pay tithes on all of his personal and business monies.

The Colonel was "always the preacher's friend." He supported many pastors. He helped many churches in their financial struggles. He had heard thousands of sermons. Yet he didn't know the Lord.

Colonel Sanders' testimony was: "You can join the church, you can serve on committees, you can be baptized and receive communion, you can become superintendent of the Sunday School, and not be saved. I know, it happened in my life. I needed to know something deep within my soul. There is an inner experience, a new birth, that brings peace. Morality and good works cannot accomplish it, it is the work of the Holy Spirit."

At age 75, he came to understand that tithing and good works would not take him to heaven. After attending a service in Louisville, Sanders walked the isle, expressing concern about his condition and the fact that, "I have lived my whole life as a Christian, and yet have never even gained control over my own tongue and swearing."

Toward the close of that service, The Colonel bowed his head, prayed, and ask Jesus to forgive him, and to have mercy upon him. After praying, The Colonel lifted his head and told the pastor, "It is the first time in my life I have ever experienced the presence of Christ within my heart."

Chapter 9
Colonellus Senex Vale

At the request of his wife, Claudia Sanders, The Colonel's funeral was held in the Alumni Memorial Chapel at Southern Seminary.

Pat Boone participated in the service and sang "What a Friend We Have in Jesus" and "He Touched Me."

Scripture readings and the primary meditation were delivered by two of Sanders' retired pastors, J. Edward Cayce and John S. Chambers.

The audio and official program from Colonel Sanders' funeral service in Alumni Chapel can be downloaded at:

https://repository.sbts.edu/handle/10392/4916

Conclusion

So what was the message that had such a profound impact on Colonel Sanders at the end of his life?

It was a simple one:

All Have Sinned.

> ***Romans 3:10*** states, ***"As it is written, There is none righteous, no, not one."***
>
> And again in ***Romans 3:23*** we are told, ***"For all have sinned, and come short of the glory of God."***
>
> ***Romans 5:12*** tells us, ***"Wherefore, as by one man [Adam] sin entered into the world, and death by sin; and so death passed upon all men, for that all have sinned."***
>
> When Adam sinned, he brought the curse of sin upon all mankind. This is why everyone is born with a nature to sin, it has been passed down since Adam.

There is a Penalty for Sin.

> ***Romans 6:23*** says, ***"For the wages of sin is death; but the gift of God is eternal life through Jesus Christ our Lord."***

Death is the penalty for sin, Physical Death and a *Second Death*. Most people confuse spiritual death with the *Second Death*.

We are born spiritually-dead. Adam and Eve died spiritually the moment they sinned, and every one of their descendants since have been born spiritually-dead. This is why a person must be born-again spiritually.

God's Holy Spirit is that spiritual life.

The Bible also speaks of a *Second Death*, being cast into the Lake of Fire forever as punishment for our sins.

Just as a person is paid wages for work performed on the job, so does God payback sinners in the Lake of Fire.

Jesus Died, Was Buried, And Rose Three Days Later.

Romans 5:8, "God commendeth his love toward us, in that, while we were yet sinners, Christ died for us."

What a precious Scripture! God in His love decided to give mankind a chance to escape the wrath of God's judgment. Jesus came and laid down

His life for us, knowing just how sinful the human race is. God expressed His love for humanity, paying men's sin debt, knowing that we are so undeserving.

Call Upon the Lord Jesus to Be Saved.

Romans 10:13 promises, ***"For whosoever shall call upon the name of the Lord shall be saved."***

The word "call" means "to appeal unto."

Lost sinners who come to Jesus for forgiveness of sins, believing that He is the Christ, the Son of God, will be saved.

How much faith do you need to be saved? Just enough faith to obey Romans 10:13 and trust upon the Lord Jesus for salvation.

Romans 10:9-10, "That if thou shalt confess with thy mouth the Lord Jesus, and shalt believe in thine heart that God hath raised him from the dead, thou shalt be saved. For with the heart man believeth unto righteousness; and with the mouth confession is made unto salvation."

To learn more about what the Bible says about
salvation you can eMail me:

president@bibleschool.edu

28

https://www.amazon.com/dp/B00KOB42E0

The Christian Testimony of
General Robert E. Lee

Edward R. DeVries, Ph.D.

https://www.amazon.com/dp/B00KMW0EGG

https://www.amazon.com/dp/B00KO8URLK

https://www.amazon.com/dp/B07YP2FS8P

BIOGRAPHICAL SKETCHES

of 130 men who greatly influenced fundamentalism

Compiled and Edited by
Edward R. DeVries, Th.D.

https://www.amazon.com/dp/B00VWJPAHQ

What does the Bible Teach?

Dr. Edward DeVries

https://www.amazon.com/dp/B00KN2PVJ0